A Taste of Thanksgiving
By Christopher Forest
Edited by Melissa Forest

Dear readers,

Thanks so much for reading this edition of Outhouse Books. In *A Taste of Thanksgiving*, we present unique anecdotes about that all American holiday, Thanksgiving.

Hopefully you enjoy this brand of specialized reader. It is designed for those of you who like to have a sense of accomplishment, but have limited time to read. These quick readers can be completed in one session….even in the privacy of your own "outhouse."

We hope you enjoy! Happy reading!!!

Sincerely,
The Outhouse Staff

Outhouse Books

This book takes no responsibility for the claims made by way of the research conducted to complete it.
Outhouse Books also acknowledges all trademark rights to items mentioned in this text, including:
Snoopy™, Macy's™, and Gimbels™

Summary: A collection of interesting facts, trivia, and tidbits about Thanksgiving.
Author: Christopher Forest
Editor: Melissa Forest

ISBN: 1481021109
Outhouse Books
Danvers, MA 01923
1 2 3 4 5 6 7 8 9 0 1

Clipart is in public domain courtesy of www.wpclipart.com.
We highly recommend this site which is the source of quality pictures and managed in accordance with protecting rights of image makers and the public domain.

Thanksgivings Firsts

"On Thanksgiving day, we acknowledge our dependence."
 - William Jennings Bryan"

The Pilgrims are known for celebrating the most famous Thanksgiving in American history. It was a three- day affair commemorating a successful harvest of 1621, celebrated by the surviving Pilgrims. It however was not the first American Thanksgiving.

An earlier Thanksgiving was held in the Jamestown colony. In 1609, after colonies and supplies dwindled, the settlers of the colony celebrated the first Thanksgiving in the thirteen original colonies. Another one was held in the colony in 1612, and a thanksgiving celebration was also held in nearby Barkley Plantation in 1619.

An even earlier Thanksgiving was held in the British colonies – though not one of the original thirteen at the time. In 1586, British settlers in the original settlement of Roanoke (a predecessor of the later settlement made famous as the Lost Colony) of 100 men had put up with many hardships in the New World. When a supply ship arrived, they celebrated a day of Thanksgiving…and soon after were so thankful they decided to abandon the colony and return home.

In 1564, French Huguenots settling in Florida celebrated an early Thanksgiving. On June 30th of that year, they gave thanks for successfully settling in Jacksonville. Sadly, a year later, their settlement was taken over by Spanish settlers.

An even earlier Thanksgiving – the first held in what is the United States, occurred in 1541. In that year, explorers with Spanish conquistador Francisco Coronado, celebrated a Thanksgiving feast during the search for the fabled city of gold in the southwestern United States. It was held in the Palo Duro Canyon in what is now the Texas Panhandle.

The first probable American Thanksgiving occurred in 1513. In that year, Spanish explorer Juan Ponce de Leon most likely celebrated a Thanksgiving celebration while exploring Florida.

The Puritans of Massachusetts were not known as a festive people, but they did know how to celebrate a good religious holiday when they wanted. They celebrated a Thanksgiving in 1630, the year they settled Trimountaine…later known as Boston.

Canada's first Thanksgiving occurred in 1578. Explorer Martin Frobisher declared the holiday upon his crew's safe arrival from England to Newfoundland.

On June 29, 1671, the citizens of Charlestown, Massachusetts celebrated a Thanksgiving holiday. It was the first publicly recorded celebration of the holiday in America (by proclamation of the local town council).

The first store to hold a thanksgiving parade was Philadelphia based Gimbel's department store. Their parade was held in 1920, four years before the first Macy's parade.

Thanksgiving started as a national holiday with the help of Sarah Hale. This editor of Lady Godey's Book, a magazine of the day, used her editorial prowess to help advance the idea. She hand wrote letters to many presidents of the day, with little response. However, when her letter reached the desk of president Abraham Lincoln, he took to the idea in 1863. A national holiday was soon born. You may not have heard of her, but you probably know something she wrote… a little ditty called "Mary Had a Little Lamb."

The year of two Thanksgivings? In 1863, President Abraham Lincoln declared the November thanksgiving as a national holiday. However, it was a year with two thanksgivings. The president had actually declared a Thanksgiving earlier that year, following the Battle of Gettysburg.

Abraham Lincoln may have started the first official national Thanksgiving, but presidents George Washington, John Adams, and James Madison all recommended that Americans celebrate the day.

Thanks for everything

A big key to thanksgiving is to – of course – "give thanks." List three things you are thankful for.

1.

2.

3.

Wampanoag's World and Pilgrims Progress

"Who does not thank for little does not thank for much."
- Estonian Proverb

The Pilgrims may have celebrated the most memorable Thanksgiving in America. However, they definitely did not call themselves Pilgrims. They believed themselves to be Separatists…separating themselves from the Anglican Church of England.

William Bradford organized the first Thanksgiving. There were 52 Pilgrims (including four women who cooked most of the food) and 90 Wampanoag Native Americans attending the feast.

Those Thanksgiving birds that are often depicted with Pilgrims in Thanksgiving decorations are incorrect for two reasons. First, there were no turkeys eaten during Thanksgiving. Second, the typical birds shown are domesticated turkeys, which are twice as large as the wild turkeys Pilgrims would have eaten.

"Our harvest being gotten in our Governor sent four men on fowling, so we might after a more special manner rejoice together, after we had gathered the fruit of our labors. They, four, in one day killed as much fowl as with a little beside, served the company almost a week. At which time amongst other recreations, we exercised our arms, many of the Indians coming amongst us, and amongst the rest their greatest King Massasoit with some 90 men, whom for three days we entertained and feasted. And they went out and killed five deer which they brought to the Plantation, and bestowed on our Governor, and upon the Captain and others."

- Edward Winslow, Pilgrim, in a letter found in *Mourt's Relations*, one of two descriptions of the first Thanksgiving in Plymouth"

Native Americans celebrate the modern Thanksgiving differently. In Plymouth, they hold a National Day of Mourning on Cole's Hill in Plymouth, which overlooks the waterfront that the Pilgrims used to enter Plymouth.

The cooperation between the Pilgrims and Wampanoag Native Americans was not just out of kindness….it was out of necessity. The Pilgrims needed help surviving and the Wampanoag needed help against their enemies that the time, the nearby Narragansett tribe.

Facts about the Pilgrims

1. The Pilgrims actually relocated to the Netherlands before coming to America. One of the reasons for coming to America is, they believed, their children were losing their British identity in the Netherlands.

2. The Pilgrims tried to settle on Cape Cod at first. However, they had difficult encounters with the Native Americans there (as had the French, who may have buried a body there that the Pilgrims discovered) and decided to settle elsewhere.

3. The region the Pilgrims settled in had been mapped by well known explorer and former Jamestown settler John Smith (he left Virginia and later returned to northern America to explore).

4. The Pilgrims fought sickness during their first year in the New World. About half of their population died as a result.

Not all of the arrivals to the New World were considered Separatists. To help finance the voyage, the Separatists had to invite other people to come to America. These people were affectionately called "the Strangers."

The Pilgrims had a patent to settle in Virginia. At the time, Virginia extended up to the Hudson River Valley (which is where the Pilgrims hoped to settle). A late start, storms, and trouble crossing the ocean accounted for the decision to remain in Massachusetts. Because they had no right to settle the region, the Pilgrims had to come up with the first form of democratic government in what is now the United States….hence the Mayflower Compact.

Neither Speedy, nor well. Although the *Mayflower* is widely known as the Pilgrim's ship, the Separatists actually departed for the New World on two ships – the *Mayflower* and the *Speedwell*. However, the *Speedwell,* proved poorly named. It lagged behind and suffered problems that delayed the voyage. About half way across, it was decided that the ship might not make it to the New World. Those that could, left the *Speedwell* and joined the *Mayflower*; hence the overcrowding on the ship.

Of buckles and black and white. Check out these popular myths of the Pilgrims:

1. They wore buckles on their hats. This is not true….only leprechauns probably did this. In fact, Pilgrims did not wear them on their shoes, either.

2. A pilgrim by any other name…the Pilgrims never referred to themselves as Pilgrims. If anything, they considered themselves Separatists.

3. What's black and white all over…not the Pilgrim attire. Though old-fashioned pictures often show the Pilgrims in black and white, their clothes were actually cheerful and colorful.

Play ball. The first thanksgiving included playing games, dancing, and singing, as well as giving thanks.

In retrospect…the first thanksgiving in Plymouth is often told in retrospect. The actual first recorded celebration of the event – at the time it happened – occurred in 1623. Most statements about the 1621 celebration are recollections by Pilgrims who were there.

The Big Three

The Big Three Native Americans who helped the Pilgrims were:

Samoset – he was a tribal leader and first made contact with them.

Squanto – he spoke English and helped the Pilgrims plant their first crops.

Massasoit – he was the elder chief of the Wampanoag tribe and created a treaty with the Pilgrims.

Squanto is well remembered for his role in helping the Pilgrims and with good reason. He had been a member of the local Patuxet tribe whose land the Pilgrims lived on. He had been captured as a slave (twice) and because of this avoided the smallpox plagued that ravaged his tribe and made the land open to settlers. He learned to speak English while a slave and was actually freed by John Smith (some sources also suggest Smith may have captured Squanto to begin with) during one of Smith's voyages to New England.

Squanto taught the Pilgrims how to use fish as fertilizer and plant beans, corn, and pumpkins together.

The Pilgrims did not stay alone in the New World for long. Three other ships soon followed, including *The Fortune* (1621) *The Anne* (1623) and *the Little James* (1623). In later years, as Plymouth grew, the Pilgrims from these four ships were called "The Old Comers" and were treated well.

Much of what we know about the Pilgrim's voyage and life comes from William Bradford. He served as governor of the colony for 30 years. He also wrote a lengthy journal about the colony and the Pilgrim arrival.

The Native Americans in the region celebrated their own versions of Thanksgiving. Some of the common Native American Thanksgivings include "The Strawberry Thanksgiving" and "The Green Corn Thanksgiving."

The reason that the Wampanoag joined the Pilgrim's Thanksgiving remains unknown. It was never written. Nor, do historians know exactly when the feast happened, only that it was between September 21 and November 9, 1621.

Party like it is 1621. The first Thanksgiving lasted three days.

During the crossing of the *Mayflower*, only one person died during the voyage. The person was a crewmember who actually scoffed at the settlers going to the New World.

The Pilgrims spent about 66 days at sea before they sighted land. They were believed to have spotted first Cape Cod. They did not venture further then Cape Cod because of the onset of winter (and the fact that the waters around Cape Cod were known to be dangerous).

Oceanus Hopkins was the first baby born to the Pilgrims. He was born during the voyage across the Great Ocean, which is how he got his name.

Want to speak like a Pilgrim?

Here's a few terms to use:

"*Good morrow*" means good morning

"*Godspeed*" means good luck

"*Arsy varsy*" means backwards

"*mouser*" means cat

"*prosperous*" means very

Pilgrims weren't the only new comers to travel on the Mayflower. Pigs, goats, and chickens did, too.

Squanto is often viewed as the savior of the Pilgrims. Indeed, he did help the Pilgrims. Yet, in his adopted tribe he is also viewed as a troublemaker, which is forgotten to history. It is believed that he tried to wrestle control of the tribe from main sachem, Massasoit. The Pilgrims had to protect Squanto.

Ever wonder what happened to the *Mayflower*? It did make its way back to England. It was eventually used as a fishing boat. By 1624, the ship was eventually scrapped and some people believe the wood was used to build barns and houses. According to legend, there is a barn in Jordans, England that some people speculate have been made from the wood of the *Mayflower*. It even has the words "Mayflower" emblazoned on the lumber framing.

One of the lesser known tragedies of the Pilgrims is the fact that future governor William Bradford's wife was lost after the Pilgrims arrived and were moored in Cape Cod Bay. In December, 1620, she apparently fell overboard. Weighted down by her heavy clothes, and possibly unable to swim, she drowned. Eventually, people speculated she committed suicide, but based on the religious beliefs of the Pilgrims – and the lack of proof in any Pilgrim writing – this is unlikely.

The Pilgrims were not part of the Massachusetts colony created by the Puritans. In fact, they tried to keep a separate colony until the 1700s.

Wash day! An old time New England tradition made Monday as wash day. People often made Monday as the day to do laundry (making a weekly day to do laundry is still common in New England). The custom dates back to the day Pilgrim women were allowed to disembark the *Mayflower* to wash clothes…which was a Monday.

Plymouth Rock

The legendary four-ton symbol of the Pilgrims has long been part of American lore. However, none of the Pilgrims ever wrote about the rock. Instead, the story of the rock comes from the relatives of Elder Faunce, one of the forefathers of the region, who spoke of the rock in 1741. He mentioned it was the site of the original Pilgrim landing and the fact was verified by a man named Deacon Spooner. However, their knowledge was second hand, from people who claimed to have landed on it. *Mourt's Relations* and William Bradford's journal do not mention the rock.

A thanksgiving blessing:

Design your own thanksgiving blessing below. Maybe it will become part of your Thanksgiving tradition

Thanksgiving Traditions

"There is only one day that is ours. Thanksgiving is the one day that is truly American."
- O Henry

The Macy's Day Thanksgiving Parade has been a staple of American tradition. The original parade in New York began in 1924 as a way for workers to celebrate the day. More than 400 workers took part in the parade. There were no big balloons, but there were live animals, like elephants and camels.

The current Macy's Day Parade extends about 2.5 miles. However, the original parade wound its way five miles through New York.

He was a high flyer! Tony Sarg is the man responsible for originally designing those wonderful hot air balloons in the Macy's Day parade. A children's book illustrator and puppeteer, his balloons went into the parades in 1927. He also made some of the first animatronic displays to appear in the store's windows as well.

Joe Cool! Snoopy has appeared as a balloon more often than any other in the Macy's day parade.

Legend has it the male turkeys are named Tom in honor of Thomas Jefferson. Rumor persists that Ben Franklin was upset that his old buddy, TJ, disagreed with his idea of having a turkey as a national bird. So, in playful banter, he supposedly called the males "Tom Turkey."

Football and thanksgiving first went joined forces in 1934. In that year, a man named G.A. Richards purchased the Detroit Lions. Hoping to promote fan interest, he scheduled a Thanksgiving Day game with the Chicago Bears, who had won the previous world championship. The game was a sell out and was broadcast on the radio. Since that day turkey and lions – Detroit Lions that is – have been a part of the Thanksgiving menu.

The first college Thanksgiving football game predates the NFL's version by decades. Princeton squared off against Yale in 1876, to mark the first college football game. Oh, and by the way, Yale won.

Thanksgiving Day – and not the day before – is the busiest travel day in the United States.

In 2001, the UP Postal Service decided to celebrate Thanksgiving as well. They unveiled the "We Give Thanks" stamp. Designed by Margaret Cusack, the stamp depicted a folk art version of a cornucopia, overflowing with fruit.

A traditional Thanksgiving

Thanksgiving is all about traditions. What are your favorite Thanksgiving traditions?

Talking Turkey

"Thanksgiving dinners take eighteen hours to prepare. They are consumed in 12 minutes. Half times take twelve minutes. This is not a coincidence."
   - Erma Bombeck

Turkeys have to be careful. They can drown when looking up at the sky during a rainstorm.

A walking heart attack waiting to happen? Yes, this can happen…to turkeys. The U.S. Air Force conducted plane tests and learned that turkeys can indeed have heart attacks. Of course, the Air Force didn't intend for this to happen. During a test flight using planes cruising at the speed of sound, an unusual event occurred. The planes flew near turkey flocks on the ground. The turkey owners, and the government, learned the hard way that turkeys get heart attacks.

Why does turkey make us sleepy? Popular stories suggest it is the chemical tryptophan, which is found in turkey and is known to cause drowsiness. However, that is probably not the source of all the tiredness. Rather, it is most likely do to the amount of food that is eaten on that day. Large quantities of food and other beverages can slow the body down. Besides, if you want a large dose of tryptophan, put a little extra parmesan on your soybeans. They both have larger quantities of tryptophan.

Gobbling up the attention. Only guy turkeys gobble. And the reason is simple – they gobble to attract a mate. No one knows what the females think of the quaint sound, but it must work. And, each male has a unique gobble.

Gobbling it up! According to at least one survey, nearly 88 percent of Americans claim they eat turkey on Thanksgiving.

Talk about embarrassing. The skin on a turkey's head and neck can change color, from its typical pink to red or blue. They color may change if a turkey is suddenly scared or angered.

Do you want to eat the most turkey? Well, head to California. Californians, by virtue of their population and size of state, eat more turkey than anyone else in the U.S.

The famous dance, the turkey trot was named for the movement of turkeys.

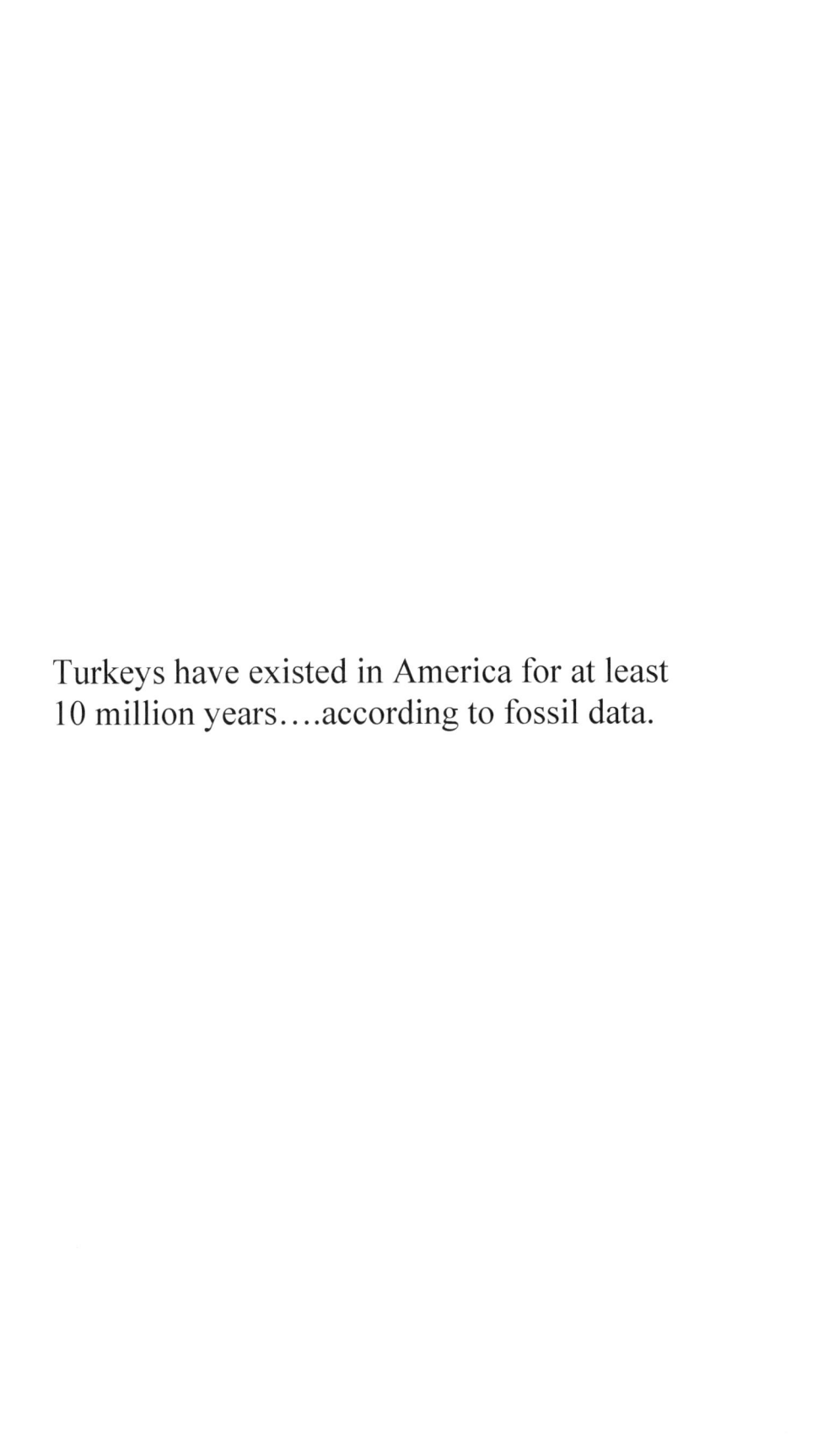

Turkeys have existed in America for at least 10 million years….according to fossil data.

Wild turkeys may weigh more than 30 pounds, but they can take to the air to escape predators such as coyotes and raccoons. Wild turkeys can fly up to 55 mph for short periods of time. In fact, turkeys often sleep in trees.

The turkeys people traditionally eat at Thanksgiving cannot fly. They have been bred for meat and are too weighed down to take to the air.

THANKGIVING JOKES

Why can't a turkey talk in public?
They use fowl language.

Why was the turkey such a fast eater?
He gobbles everything up.

Why did the police arrest the turkey?
They suspected him of fowl play.

Why did the turkey join the band?
She already had drumsticks.

Why didn't the turkey finish his dessert?
He was stuffed.

What did the turkey's cell tone sound like?
"Wing, wing"

Thanksgiving Foods

"Thanksgiving, man. It's a bad day to be my pants."
   - Kevin James

Do you want to celebrate a traditional Thanksgiving? Here's your checklist of items that are believed to have been served at the first Thanksgiving.

___ venison

___ pumpkin

___ berries

___ corn

___ turkey

___ squash

___ clams

___ eel

___ ducks and waterfowl

___ fish

About 750 million pounds of cranberries are produced in the U.S. each year. The top producers of cranberries in the U.S. are Wisconsin and Massachusetts.

Cranberries were originally called craneberries. The flowers resemble a crane's head.

Want to make sure your cranberries are fresh? Try this trick. Drop one on the ground from a short distance. High quality cranberries bounce. But, don't forget to clean them before cooking.

Cranberry sauce was not served at the original Thanksgiving. In fact, sugar, a necessary ingredient, was a scarce commodity in 1621.

Uses for Cranberries.
Prior to being a turkey day staple, cranberries had other uses.

- They were used by Native Americans as dyes.

- They were used by native Americans to treat arrow wounds.

Got the stuffing! About 50 percent of Americans love to eat original stuffing on turkey – that means stuffing placed inside the bird.

Cornucopias are a popular symbol for Thanksgiving. The original cornucopias were not made of wicker; they were made of goat horns.

Have yourself a west coast style Thanksgiving? Some people eat Dungeness crab for thanksgiving as an alternative to the gobbler. Turns out crab season begins on the west coast in November.

Love those potatoes? Take a bite out of these potato facts.

• A potato is made of 80 percent water.

• Potatoes are grown in every state of the U.S.

• The first food grown in space was a potato. In 1995, the Space Shuttle Columbia took a potato plant into space and grew it.

Potatoes seem like a long-standing tradition at Thanksgiving. However, they were not part of the original meal. They were introduced to the U.S. long after the first Thanksgiving.

You remember those delightful frozen dinners in the tinfoil package. Did you know that their invention is connected to Thanksgiving? Well, according to popular legend, the reason frozen dinners were invented by the Swanson company was they were trying to find a way to deal with left over frozen Thanksgiving turkeys. Now that's gobbling up the market.

When did the first green bean casserole become served at Thanksgiving. Well, it probably occurred around 1962. That is the year that Campbell's Soup introduced the recipe in its yearly cookbook.

The United States raises about 248 million turkeys each year. These are the main source of the turkey meals in the country. About 46 million of these end up being Thanksgiving dinner.

About 2.4 billion pounds sweet potatoes are grown each year. Many are used in the celebration of Thanksgiving. North Carolina, California, and Louisiana are top producers.

Talk about a carb load! The average American eats about 4,500 calories on Thanksgiving Day.

Thanksgiving History

"Let the thankful heart sweep through the day and, as the magnet finds the iron, so it will find, in every hour, some heavenly blessings!"
  - Henry Ward Beecher

The early forefathers were skeptical about eating turkey, in part because Benjamin Franklin held it in high regard. In fact, Alexander Hamilton came out in support of adding Turkey to any Thanksgiving meal.

In October 1863, Abraham Lincoln issued the official Thanksgiving Proclamation. In it, he set aside the last Thursday in November as the official day of Thanksgiving in this country. He found it quite fitting, particularly at the time, because the nation was in the midst of the Civil War. In fact, the Battle of Gettysburg had occurred earlier in the year.

THANKSGIVING RIDDLES

See if you can solve these riddles…all with answers that sound like "Thanksgiving"

1. What do you call a Thanksgiving celebrated with hot dogs?

2. What is a Thanksgiving held at the federal reserve?

3. What do cats call their Thanksgiving?

4. Tricksters love to celebrate this feast.

5. Grumpy guys love to eat this feast.

Answers are on the following page.

THANKSGIVING RIDDLES
Check out these answers.

1. Franksgiving

2. Banksgiving

3. Manxgiving

4. Pranksgiving

5. Cranksgiving

The date for Thanksgiving temporarily changed in 1939. Then president Franklin Delano Roosevelt changed the date to the third Thursday (November 23) instead of November 30. His reasoning was that the country was still in a depression and he wanted to extend the Christmas shopping season to spur the economy. Incidentally, many Republicans chose to celebrate it on the 30th anyway, giving rise to the year of two Thanksgivings. November 30 was Republican Thanksgiving and November 23 was Democratic Thanksgiving or Franksgiving.

The set date for Thanksgiving was voted on December 26, 1941 (ironically, the day after Christmas). It established the fourth Thursday of November as the uniform date for the national holiday.

In 1777, the 13 colonies celebrated an official national Thanksgiving. It was a one day celebration to commemorate the American victory over the British in the Battle of Freeman's Farm, (better known as the Battle of Saratoga).

The date for Canada's Thanksgiving was originally set as November 6. The law, passed in 1879, was not fully adopted by all people. So Thanksgiving Day still varied. In 1957, the country established the second Monday in October as the nation's official Thanksgiving Day.

Thomas Jefferson may not have liked the idea of the turkey as a national bird, but he liked the idea of Thanksgiving even less. He thought that a national thanksgiving day was "the most ridiculous idea ever conceived."

Thanksgiving must see TV

Five things to watch in honor of Thanksgiving

1. *Charlie Brown Thanksgiving*

2. *Squanto*

3. *The Mayflower Adventure*

4. *The Blind Side* (at the beginning, it takes place around Thanksgiving)

5. *Planes, Trains, and Automobiles* (which also takes place at Thanksgiving)

Thanksgiving Leftovers

"A thankful heart is not only the greatest virtue, but the parent of all other virtues."
- Cicero

The earliest Thanksgiving can occur is November 22 and the latest it can occur is November 28.

Each year, the National Turkey Federation presents three turkeys to the president. The custom began with Harry Truman in 1947 and continues to this day. The president receives one live turkey – which receives the official presidential pardon and will eventually spend the reminder of its life on a farm. The president also receives two dressed turkeys, which may be eaten.

Thanksgiving nicknames

- Turkey day

- Yanksgiving (said by some Canadians to distinguish it from Canadian Thanksgiving)

- Football Holiday

- T-day (for turkey)

- Macy's Day (common in New York City)

- Butterball Day

Makihiki is the Hawaiian Thanksgiving celebration that was celebrated by the original inhabitants of the island. It was a four-month celebration, from November until February. War and work were stopped during this period.

Word Search Answers

Try to find the items hidden in this word search.

m	p	t	u	r	k	e	y	s	w
i	m	a	y	f	l	o	w	e	r
r	s	e	e	s	q	u	a	u	o
g	b	e	r	n	m	e	h	i	t
l	a	p	u	a	p	e	l	b	n
i	e	l	m	e	l	l	s	t	a
p	g	e	p	b	y	k	u	r	u
o	h	t	u	o	m	y	l	p	q
i	p	i	e	o	i	e	l	s	s
p	i	p	u	m	p	k	i	n	m

beans   corn   eel   mayflower   pie   pilgrim
Plymouth   pumpkin
         Squanto   turkey

Word Search Answers

m		t	u	r	k	e	y		
i	m	a	y	f	l	o	w	e	r
r				s					o
g				n		e			t
l				a		e			n
i				e		l			a
p				b					u
		h	t	u	o	m	y	l	p	q
		p	i	e					s
			p	u	m	p	k	i	n	

beans   corn   eel   mayflower   pie   pilgrim   Plymouth   pumpkin   Squanto   turkey

AAA speculates that about 42 million people drive at least 50 miles during the Thanksgiving period to visit family.

Pilgrims probably made an early version of pumpkin pie. However, their version was made inside the pumpkin. It was cooked by hollowing out a pumpkin and filling it with milk, spice, and honey.

Want to celebrate your Thanksgiving in a town appropriately named for the holiday. Well, then check out:

Turkey, North Carolina

Turkey, Texas

Turkey Creek, Louisiana

Breaking a wishbone is a tradition some families still adhere to. Make sure the wishbone is dried before breaking. The tradition dates back to the Etruscans, who began breaking wishbones in 322 BC. The custom eventually spread through the Roman Empire.

About 84 percent of all Americans attend some type of Thanksgiving dinner. And, 94 percent of those dinners will include cranberry sauce.

In Hawaii, some people rub coffee on turkey to add flavor.

Thank New York. New York was the first state to make Thanksgiving an annual tradition in 1817.

Some stories suggest that popcorn was part of the first Thanksgiving. This is not true…though Native Americans did know how to pop corn.

How many words can you make out of the word THANKSGIVING

Leftovers!

Almost everyone loves leftovers. What are your favorite leftover recipes? List them here:

From all of us
To all of you
We wish you a very happy,
Healthy, and blessed
Thanksgiving

Happy Thanksgiving

This book is dedicated to the Cooke family – our family members and original settlers to Plymouth – who helped inspire our love of all things Thanksgiving.

Sources:

"Fun Thanksgiving Facts and Trivia." *Reluctant Gourmet*. URL: http://www.reluctantgourmet.com/blog/all-about-cooking/thanksgiving-facts-trivia/

"Homework Help." *Plymouth Plantation*. URL: http://www.plimoth.org/learn/just-kids/homework-help

"Thanksgiving Facts". *WHSV TV*. URL: http://www.whsv.com/seasonal/misc/33852054.html

"Thanksgiving Facts." *History.com*. URL http://www.history.com/topics/thanksgiving-facts

"Thanksgiving Facts" *Random History.Com.* URL: http://facts.randomhistory.com/thanksgiving-facts.html

"Thanksgiving Facts and Trivia" http://suite101.com/article/thanksgiving-facts-and-trivia-a307091

"Thanksgiving Trivia: 11 Facts You Should Know" *Huffington Post.* URL: http://www.huffingtonpost.com/2011/11/21/thanksgiving-trivia-facts_n_1106005.html#s489257&title=How_Did_The

"36 Little Known Thanksgiving Facts" "Plymouth Rock," *Pilgrim* Hall. URL: http://www.pilgrimhall.org/Rock.htm

"Common Mayflower and Pilgrim Myths." http://www.mayflowerhistory.com/Introduction/commonmyths.php

"Coolest Thanksgiving Facts" http://www.coolest-holiday-parties.com/thanksgiving-facts.html

"The First Thanksgiving" National Geographic for Kids. URL: http://kids.nationalgeographic.com/kids/stories/history/first-thanksgiving/

Fun Thanksgiving and Deep Thoughts. *Prospectmx*. URL: http://www.prospectmx.com/fun-thanksgiving-facts-deep-thoughts/

"Thanksgiving Timeline." *Local.gov*. URL: http://www.loc.gov/teachers/classroommaterials/presentationsandactivities/presentations/thanksgiving/timeline/1564.html

Made in the USA
Middletown, DE
29 October 2021